UNCOVERING HISTORY

THE AZTECS, INCAS, & MAYA

Everyday Life of the Aztecs, Incas, and Maya
was created and produced by McRae Books
Borgo Santa Croce, 8 – Florence (Italy)
e-mail: info@mcraebooks.com

SERIES EDITOR Anne McRae
TEXT Neil Morris
ILLUSTRATIONS Manuela Cappon, Luisa Della Porta, Paola Ravaglia, Andrea Ricciardi di
Gaudesi, Studio Stalio (Alessandro Cantucci, Fabiano Fabbrucci, Andrea Morandi)
GRAPHIC DESIGN Marco Nardi
LAYOUT Laura Ottina, Adriano Nardi
EDITING Vicky Egan
REPRO Litocolor, Florence
PICTURE RESEARCH Anne McRae

Published in the United States by Smart Apple Media
1980 Lookout Drive, North Mankato, Minnesota 56003

Printed and bound in Italy

Library of Congress Cataloging-in-Publication Data
Morris, Neil.
Everyday life of the Aztecs, Incas, and Maya / by Neil Morris ; illustrated by Manuela Cappon,
Luisa Della Porta, Andrea Ricciardi di Gaudesi.
p. cm. — (Uncovering history)
Originally published: Florence, Italy : McRae Books, c2003.
Includes index.
Contents: Mesoamerican origins — Mayan agriculture — Mayan society — Mayan religion — A
Mayan temple — Mayan calendar and writing system — Daily life among the Maya — Rise of the
Aztecs — Daily life in an Aztec village — Aztec religion — Aztec life and rituals — Before the Incas
— Incan burial — Incan religion — Incan roads and trade — Incan farmers — Life in the
mountains — The Inca empire — The conquest of the Americas.
ISBN 1-58340-253-5
1. Mayas—Juvenile literature. 2. Aztecs—Juvenile literature. 3. Incas—Juvenile literature. [1.
Mayas. 2. Aztecs. 3. Incas. 4. Indians of Central America. 5. Indians of Mexico. 6. Indians of South
America.] I. Cappon, Manuela. II. Della Porta, Luisa. III. Ricciardi, Andrea. IV. Title. V. Series.

F1435.G72 2003
972'.0009'031—dc21   2003042350

First Edition
9 8 7 6 5 4 3 2 1

UNCOVERING HISTORY

Neil Morris

EVERYDAY LIFE OF THE
AZTECS, INCAS, & MAYA

Illustrations by Manuela Cappon, Luisa Della Porta, Studio Inklink, Andrea Ricciardi di Gaudesi, Studio Stalio

Smart Apple Media

Table of Contents

Introduction

People first migrated to Central America and the Andean region of South America many thousands of years ago. When they settled and took up farming, these early Americans created many different cultures. In Mesoamerica, the Maya formed the most successful civilization between A.D. 250 and 900. But they were not alone. The earlier Olmecs had made colossal statues of their rulers, while other groups built the great cities of Monte Alban and Teotihuacan. After the decline of the Maya, the Toltecs came to the fore. In the 12th century, the Aztecs moved south and built their fabulous capital in central Mexico.

Further south, in the Andes mountains around present-day Peru, the civilizations of the Chavin, Nazca, Moche, and others rose and fell. Then another group developed and built a spectacular empire—the Incas. Before the end of the 15th century, Europeans knew little or nothing about the great civilizations of the Americas. But tales of gold and fabulous wealth soon attracted Spanish conquerors, who arrived in the New World in the early 1500s. Their guns and steel swords helped them to quickly destroy the empires of the Incas and the Aztecs.

Many of the pyramid-temples, tombs, and cities of these great civilizations were left to crumble, and some disappeared as jungle reclaimed the land. Then explorers and archaeologists began uncovering the remains and piecing together the lives of ordinary people, as well as their rulers.

Chronology of the Pre-Columbian World

EARLY PRE-CLASSIC PERIOD
IN MESOAMERICA
2000–1000 B.C.

MIDDLE PRE-CLASSIC PERIOD
1000–400 B.C.

Maya settle in the Yucatan and Guatemala c. 1000 B.C.
Chavin culture in South America c. 900–200 B.C.

LATE PRE-CLASSIC PERIOD
400 B.C.–A.D. 250

Maya start building temples c. 400 B.C.
Nazca culture flourishes 200 B.C.-A.D. 700
Teotihuacan founded c. 200 B.C.

EARLY CLASSIC PERIOD
IN MESOAMERICA
A.D. 250–600

LATE CLASSIC PERIOD
600–909

EARLY POST-CLASSIC PERIOD
IN MESOAMERICA 909–1200

Aztecs move toward Valley of Mexico c. 1100
First Inca emperor founds Cuzco c. 1100

LATE POST-CLASSIC PERIOD
1200–1697

Spanish conquerors destroy Tenochtitlan and Aztec empire 1521

Inca empire collapses 1536

Mesoamerican Origins

The original inhabitants of Mesoamerica (or "Middle America") wandered the region hunting animals, gathering plants, and fishing along the coasts. These were people of the pre-classic period of Mesoamerican civilization, which lasted from 2000 B.C. to A.D. 250. Around 1000 B.C., some settled in the rainforests of the Yucatan Peninsula of Mexico and the northern part of present-day Guatemala. By that time the Olmec civilization, on the Gulf Coast, already included ceremonial centers and huge sculptures. Their ideas and customs spread far beyond the Olmec homeland and greatly influenced the developing Mayan society. People on the lowland coast wanted rocks and precious stones from the highlands for building and carving sculptures. Those in the highlands wanted salt, honey, and cacao, which the lowlanders could provide. This led to a great trade network across the growing city-states of the region.

→ Migrations

Bands of hunter-gatherers made their way over the Bering Strait from Asia around 17,000 years ago. Moving south, they populated all regions of North and South America.

This early Mesoamerican plate with a fish design originally stood on four legs.

Maya area
Aztec area
Aztec heartland

Mayan territory covered much of southern and eastern Mexico, as well as Belize, Guatemala, and parts of Honduras and El Salvador. The Olmec culture developed near the Gulf of Mexico, while the Zapotecs were further south, near the Pacific coast. Teotihuacan is in central Mexico, near modern-day Mexico City.

• Chichen Itza

Teotihuacan •

GULF OF MEXICO

San Lorenzo • • La Venta

Monte Alban •

• Bonampak

• Copán

This stone figurine was found at a sacrificial site at Uaxactun, in present-day Guatemala. It dates from the late pre-classic period.

Early Maya

The earliest Mayan farming villages developed around 1000 B.C., in the lowlands of northern Guatemala. Over the next few hundred years, the Maya settled throughout the lowland regions of the Yucatan. The settlers lived in small villages made up of simple, thatched houses. Around 400 B.C., they started to build temples, where they could worship their many gods. As their population grew, separate city-states developed, each with its own Mayan ruler.

The Olmecs

The Olmecs of the Gulf Coast region built towns around ceremonial centers soon after 1200 B.C. Two of their most famous centers were San Lorenzo and La Venta. The Olmecs made beautiful figurines from serpentine and jade, but they are most famous for their giant stone heads. They used sledges and rafts to transport basalt boulders from nearby mountains. They then carved them into heads (below), whose features probably represented their rulers.

The Zapotecs

The Zapotecs founded their capital city of Monte Alban in the mountainous Oaxaca region around 500 B.C. They levelled off the top of a mountain before building a ceremonial center around a Great Plaza, with palaces, temples, and tombs. They also made flat terraces on the hillsides around the city, for farmers to grow their crops. The early Zapotecs must have had contact with the late Olmecs.

A clay vessel in the form of a jaguar, which was a symbol of universal power among the Zapotecs and other Central American peoples.

A reconstruction of Teotihuacan, looking south down the Street of the Dead (also named by the Aztecs) from the Pyramid of the Moon. To the left of the street is the Pyramid of the Sun, a temple platform which was 250 feet (75 m) high.

Teotihuacan

The ancient city of Teotihuacan was later found and named by the Aztecs. In their language, the name meant "place of the gods." The city was founded as a small settlement around 200 B.C., and it became the heart of a large trading network. Its buildings were laid out in a grid pattern, and by A.D. 500, about 200,000 people were living there. Two hundred years later, much of the city was burned, and it lost power and influence.

Above: The design of this ceremonial incense-burner is typical of Teotihuacan culture.

Farming methods

In the rainforest, the Maya used stone axes and blades of obsidian and flint to cut down trees and bushes, before burning them to make clearings. The ashes that were left behind were good for the soil, which was planted with seeds ready for the rainy season. In other areas, the Maya dug canals to bring water from nearby rivers and swamps to their crops growing in raised fields. On sloping land, the Maya made flat terraces for their fields, which they surrounded with walls.

Crops grown

Maize, beans, and squash (below) were the most important Mayan crops. Early farmers grew only enough food for their families, but later they also grew cotton and cacao trees, which were useful for trade. In their villages, the Maya had gardens, where they grew all sorts of tropical fruits, including papayas, sapodillas, and avocados. Sweet potatoes and chili peppers were also grown.

Clearing the forest for slash-and-burn agriculture was hard work. Some of the tallest trees were probably left standing. The burned fields were fertile for only one or two years, so new areas had to be cleared every year.

Mayan Farmers

Most Mayan people were farmers. The way in which they worked and the methods they used depended on their surroundings. In the rainforest, people had to clear land, while those living in dry, open country found ways of watering their fields. This was important in parts of the Yucatan Peninsula, where there are few rivers. The Maya had no horses or cattle to pull or carry heavy loads, so there was a great deal of hard work to do. Many farmers had their own plot of land, and in each village there was communal land, which everyone helped look after. The men and older boys did most of the farmwork, clearing fields, planting seeds, and harvesting crops. They also went hunting and fishing, while the women looked after the home and children, as well as prepared and cooked food.

This clay plate shows a Mayan woman using a handstone to grind maize.

Types of food

Maize (also called corn) formed the main part of most meals. The Maya used maize to make a kind of porridge spiced with chili. They also ate tamales—maize husks filled with a mixture of seasoned meat and corn dough—and the flat maize pancakes that the Spanish later called tortillas. These are still very popular in Mexico today. The Maya also used maize to make an alcoholic drink called balche, which was sweetened with honey and spiced with tree bark.

Hunting and fishing

Mayan men used the bow and arrow to hunt wild animals such as deer, monkeys, rabbits, and the piglike peccary. Snares were also set to trap nocturnal creatures such as armadillos and tapirs. Hunters shot pellets from blowguns to bring down birds such as partridges, quails, and ducks. At the coast, as well as in lakes and rivers, fishermen used both nets and hooks to make their catch.

This figurine from around A.D. 700 shows a huntsman slaying a deer.

Domestication

The Maya caught wild birds and raised them on their farms for food. These included turkeys (left), doves, and ducks. The Maya kept dogs as hunting companions, but certain breeds were also fattened and eaten. Farmers may also have kept small herds of deer in pens. They certainly raised bees, which they kept in hollow logs closed up with mud, and used the honey to sweeten food.

Eating

The main meal of the day was usually in the late afternoon, when the men had returned from the fields or the hunt. Women were responsible for preparing, cooking, and serving food, which took up a large part of their day. The men of the family ate first, followed by the women and girls. Tortillas left over from the main meal were eaten for breakfast the next day.

A container for chocolate from around A.D. 500. The Maya ground cacao seeds into a paste and then mixed it with hot water to make drinking chocolate.

Mayan Writing

Much has been learned about the Maya because they developed their own system of hieroglyphic writing. They made books and carved inscriptions on buildings and monuments. Unfortunately, their folded bark books did not last long, and most were destroyed after the Spanish conquest. Many inscriptions in soft limestone were also washed away through the centuries by the annual rainy season. Those that were left and then rediscovered were difficult for modern historians to decipher. Historians have learned to read many of them only during the past 50 years.

The Maya also had their own number system. To record dates, they used two separate calendars, which gave a different name to each day, but came together once every 52 years.

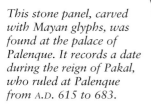

This stone panel, carved with Mayan glyphs, was found at the palace of Palenque. It records a date during the reign of Pakal, who ruled at Palenque from A.D. 615 to 683.

The glyphs on this third-century vase represent some of the named days of the ritual calendar.

This stone slab comes from Monte Alban, the capital of the Zapotecs. The earliest Mesoamerican writing was found there, dating back to about 500 B.C. The figure shown here may have been a victim of war. Other slabs record the names of surrounding provinces that the Zapotecs claimed to have conquered.

Calendars

The Maya had two calendars. The first was based on the orbit of the earth around the sun and was made up of 365 days. This Mayan year was divided into 18 months of 20 days each, with five extra days at the end—which the Maya thought were very unlucky. The second calendar was a sacred almanac of 260 days. It was based on 20 differently named days, and each was combined with a number from 1 to 13.

Hieroglyphs

Mayan writing was made up of symbols, called hieroglyphs. Some symbols were word signs, while others stood for combinations of syllables and sounds. It is thought that the Maya covered their cities with hieroglyphs, carved into the stone of buildings. They kept records on large, upright stone monuments, called stelae. The stelae noted important dates and great events in the lives of Mayan rulers.

Codices

The Maya wrote on thin strips of fig tree bark. They carefully folded the bark into a concertina to make pages. These Mayan books are called codices, but unfortunately only four of them still exist. They contain astronomical tables, information on lucky days for planting and hunting, and instructions for religious ceremonies.

A Mayan codex. The glyphs were read in columns, from top to bottom and left to right.

Arithmetic

The Mayan number system was based on 20. To write numbers, the Maya used a system of dots and bars. A dot stood for 1, and a bar for 5. To make sums easier, the Maya invented a number zero, which they represented with a shell. There was also a system of glyphs which took the form of heads (right).

Scribes

Mayan scribes performed a very important function and were held in high regard. They were specially trained to understand and then write the hundreds of Mayan hieroglyphs. Only priests and nobles could read what the scribes wrote, though ordinary people may have learned some of the most common glyphs. The scribes used brushes and quills made from turkey feathers to write on bark, and they also inscribed walls and ceramic vessels.

Astronomy

Mayan priests were also astronomers. They probably used pairs of crossed sticks or similar sighting devices to note the position of stars from the tops of temples. They observed the position of the sun, moon, and stars, calculating accurately how long it took for the moon to go around the earth and the earth to go around the sun. Astronomers made tables of solar eclipses so that they could predict when eclipses would happen in the future.

On this panel, the planet Venus appears in a star shape. Astronomers made detailed studies of the movements of Venus, which they called the "great star."

This statuette shows a Mayan woman with a codex book. Sources led historians to believe that all Mayan scribes were men, but perhaps this was not the case.

The codex-style picture on this terracotta plate shows a scribe at work.

This artist is carving a stone monument called a stele, which the Maya used to record important events.

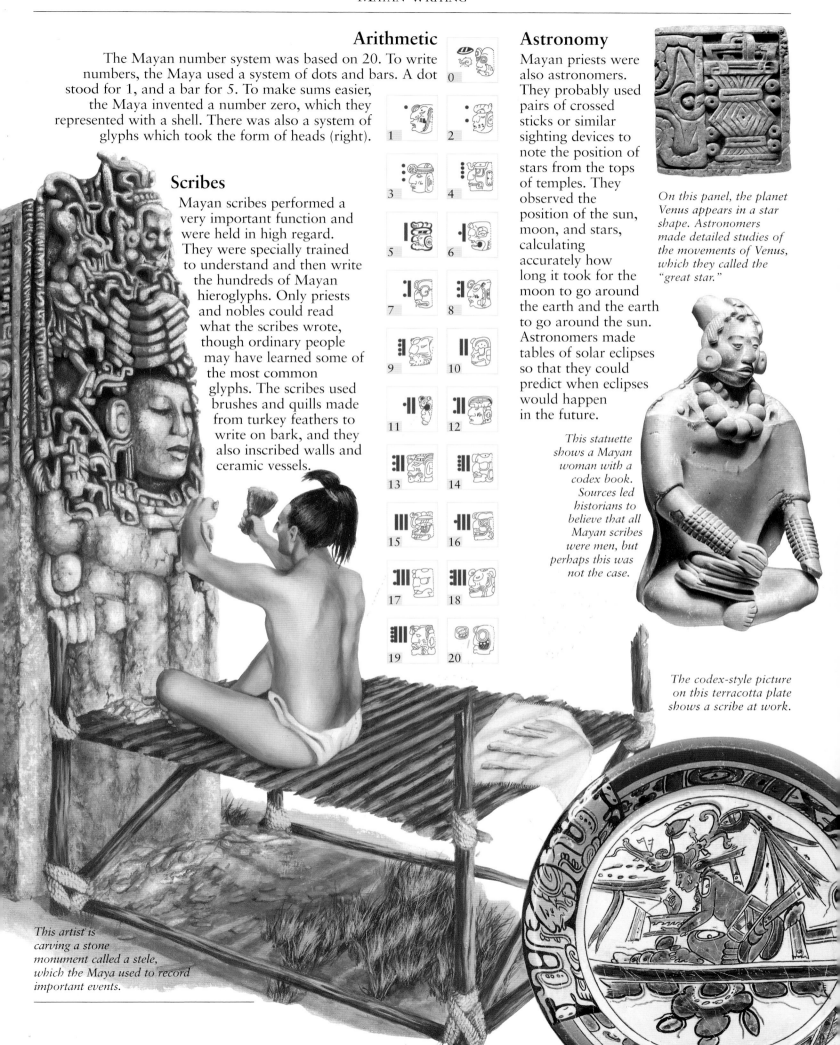

Mayan Religion

The Maya believed that all natural objects, such as trees and rocks, were inhabited by spirits with invisible powers. They worshipped a range of gods, who took the form of humans or animals. They believed that the Sun God rose every day and crossed the sky, before descending beneath the earth at night, where he became a fierce jaguar. The earth itself was the back of a giant turtle, and at its center stood a sacred kapok tree which held up the sky. But the Maya believed that theirs was not the first world. Others had existed before and been destroyed by floods, as the current world would be at the end of its allotted time.

This clay vase shows a figure emerging from a shell. Shells were thought to represent fertility, birth, and life.

Gods and goddesses

The Maya worshipped many different gods and goddesses. Among the most important were Itzamna ("Lizard House"), who was supposed to have invented writing and became the patron of learning, and his wife, Ix Chel ("Lady Rainbow"), the goddess of weaving and childbirth. Like all the other deities, the supreme god and goddess had several different aspects. The Sun God, for example, may have been one aspect of Itzamna. Individual gods were even associated with the numbers 0 to 13.

Shamans and priests

The Maya had great belief in the power of spirits to influence their everyday lives. Their early shamans, or medicine men, had close contact with the spiritual world. It was believed that shamans could drive out evil spirits, heal the sick, and use their spiritual calendar to forecast the best times to plant crops or hunt. As Mayan cities grew, these spiritual leaders joined a ruling class of priests. The chief priest and shaman of each Mayan community was the ruler himself.

Statuette of a shaman wearing the mask of a water bird. Costumes and masks such as this may have been worn at ritual ceremonies.

Mythology

The Maya believed that the present world began with a pair of Hero Twins, who were the children of previous twins from an earlier world. Their fathers had been sacrificed to the gods of death after a sacred ball game. The new Hero Twins defeated the lords of the underworld and became the main "stars" in the sky—the sun and Venus. They were the sacred role models for earthly Mayan rulers.

This incense burner shows Itzamna as an old man with a beaked nose. As the lord of the heavens, Itzamna was thought to have named all the Mayan settlements and cities.

During some celebrations, the Maya drank a great deal of alcohol and took mind-altering drugs. They believed that these activities would bring them closer to the gods.

On this eighth-century plate, the Hero Twins (to the right and left) bring the Maize God back to life. The Maize God is seen emerging from the earth, which has the shape of a turtle shell.

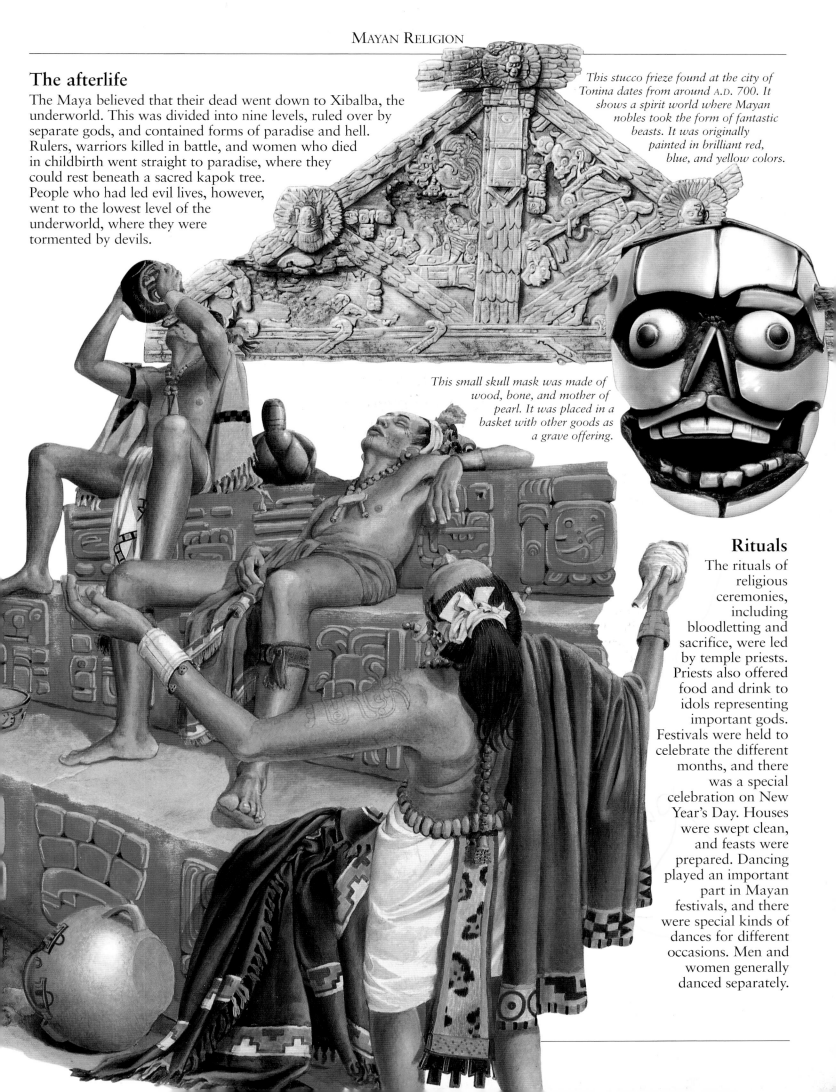

The afterlife

The Maya believed that their dead went down to Xibalba, the underworld. This was divided into nine levels, ruled over by separate gods, and contained forms of paradise and hell. Rulers, warriors killed in battle, and women who died in childbirth went straight to paradise, where they could rest beneath a sacred kapok tree. People who had led evil lives, however, went to the lowest level of the underworld, where they were tormented by devils.

This stucco frieze found at the city of Tonina dates from around A.D. 700. It shows a spirit world where Mayan nobles took the form of fantastic beasts. It was originally painted in brilliant red, blue, and yellow colors.

This small skull mask was made of wood, bone, and mother of pearl. It was placed in a basket with other goods as a grave offering.

Rituals

The rituals of religious ceremonies, including bloodletting and sacrifice, were led by temple priests. Priests also offered food and drink to idols representing important gods. Festivals were held to celebrate the different months, and there was a special celebration on New Year's Day. Houses were swept clean, and feasts were prepared. Dancing played an important part in Mayan festivals, and there were special kinds of dances for different occasions. Men and women generally danced separately.

A Mayan Temple

Mayan cities, such as Copán (in present-day Honduras), were built around ceremonial centers, which contained royal palaces and temple pyramids. Only priests were allowed to walk up to the chamber at the top of the pyramids, where they worshipped their gods and performed sacred rituals. Many rituals were based on offering blood to the gods, to please them and help them keep the world in balance. Priests may also have made astronomical observations from this great height. Modern archaeologists have discovered that many Mayan pyramids contain the tombs of kings, queens, and nobles. They were also built on top of smaller temples and shrines, which were used to honor important ancestors.

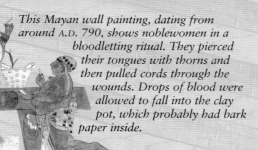

This Mayan wall painting, dating from around A.D. 790, shows noblewomen in a bloodletting ritual. They pierced their tongues with thorns and then pulled cords through the wounds. Drops of blood were allowed to fall into the clay pot, which probably had bark paper inside.

What people did in temples

Many of the rituals at temples and inside palaces involved offering blood to the gods. Animals and humans were sacrificed. Many human victims were enemies captured in war. Some were rolled down the steps of a pyramid, while others were hurled from a great height onto a pile of stones. Noblemen and noblewomen also offered their own blood, piercing themselves with spines or sharp, stone blades. Kings and queens spattered their blood onto pieces of bark paper, which were then burned in a ceremonial fire.

Mayan pyramids

Mayan temple pyramids were built up over many years, as one structure was placed around and on top of another. Most pyramids were made of blocks of limestone, then dressed with plaster and painted. At Copán, however, a local volcanic rock was used. At the top of the pyramid was a simple platform sanctuary. This had a single ritual chamber, though some temples had three connecting chambers and a crest-shaped roof comb on top.

On one pyramid at Copán, the flight of steps leading up to the sanctuary was inscribed with hieroglyphs that listed the dynasty of rulers of the kingdom.

The acropolis at Copán

Copán was at the southern end of the Mayan region, in present-day Honduras near the border of Guatemala. The first ruler of Copán founded the city beside a river in the fifth century. At its height, Copán probably had a population of around 20,000. To the north (on the left of the plan) was a Great Plaza, surrounded by altars, stelae, and a ball court. To the south was a man-made hill, or acropolis, on which there were several large temples. Sixteen rulers of Copán continued building structures, many on top of previous ones, until the city fell into decline around A.D. 800.

Chacmools

The reclining stone chacmool figure (right) clasps a stone plate between his hands. This was probably used for receiving offerings to the gods, including human hearts. The chacmools that have been found, such as those at Chichen Itza in Mexico, date from the later Mayan period.

Mayan Society

This jade mosaic vessel is thought to show Yikin Chan Kawiil, who ruled Tikal from A.D. 734 to 746. He is portrayed in the form of the god of maize.

Kingship

Mayan rulers were called "holy lords." They acted like kings and were worshipped by their subjects as if they were gods. When a ruler died, power usually passed to his eldest son. Queens were not unknown, however. When the king of Palenque, Kan Balam, died without a male heir in 583, he was succeeded by his daughter, Lady Yohl Iknal. Among the Maya, there was no single capital city and no overall king.

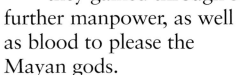

Mayan rulers lived in stone palaces near the ceremonial centers of their cities, along with their courtiers and servants. They had complete control over the surrounding villages and farmlands. A class of nobles helped the rulers govern their city-states, and warriors helped defend the city-states against other Mayan groups. In this way, the larger cities, such as Copán and Tikal, developed wealth and power throughout the classic period. The prisoners they gained through successful battles provided further manpower, as well as blood to please the Mayan gods.

Each city had its own symbol, called an emblem glyph. These symbols were used by rulers in inscriptions. The Tikal glyph (top left) actually reads "Divine Tikal Lord."

City-states

The cities and surrounding areas ruled over by kings varied in size. Some, such as Bonampak, were small towns and may have come under the power of other states. Others, such as Copán and Palenque, were large. The center of Tikal, the largest Mayan site yet discovered, covered nearly five square miles (12 sq km), but its power stretched much further than that, and its people numbered up to 70,000.

After a ruler's warriors had won a battle over another city-state, prisoners of war were brought before him. All the prisoners had to pay homage. Some were forced to spill blood for the god-king, while others paid with their lives.

The family

The basic unit of Mayan society was the family. Marriage was an important institution, and the family name and possessions were passed from father to children. When he married, a young man went to live for some years in the house of his wife's parents. He then set up his own house near his father's. This system bound families together.

This musical whistle takes the shape of a happy couple. It was found at Copán and dates from around A.D. 700.

This clay statuette of a noblewoman shows her wearing elaborate clothes and a necklace with pendants. She is also carrying a fan.

Structure of society

Aside from the kings, the ruling class of the Maya was made up of noblemen and noblewomen. Nobles had private lands and country estates, and in addition to attending the royal court, they held important positions on governing councils. High-ranking warriors and priests were also important members of society.

Warfare

The Mayan city-states sometimes went to war with each other. This may have been done to gain territory, but usually the goal was to gain prisoners, who could be put to work as slaves or, more importantly, sacrificed to the gods. Kings led their forces into battle, and to be taken captive was the worst thing that could happen to a Mayan ruler. Even the mightiest cities could fall, as happened to Tikal in 562, when it was overrun by fearsome warriors—probably from the city of Calakmul. It took Tikal a century to recover from this great defeat.

Long, heavy spears are the main weapons in this scene from a painted Mayan cylinder vase.

Mayan Daily Life

Everyday life must have been much the same in most Mayan villages. While the men went off to tend the fields, the women stayed at home to weave, cook, and look after the children. Young people's appearances were changed by various means to make them beautiful to Mayan eyes. Babies' heads were gently pressed between boards to give them a flattened appearance, and beads were hung in front of the babies' faces to make their eyes cross. When the children were older, their front teeth were filed, and after marriage they often had their bodies tattooed. As Mayan cities developed, however, life began to change for the families of scribes, craftworkers, and merchants.

Village life

Mayan families, including grandparents, parents, and children, lived together in small villages near their fields. The walls of their simple houses were made of wooden poles lashed together and covered with mud. The roof was thatched with palm leaves or grass, and was steeply sloped so that rainwater ran off easily. One half of the house was used for cooking and eating, with a firepit in the middle of the floor. The family slept in the other half on raised beds made from wood and woven bark.

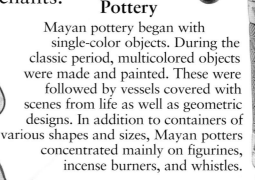

(Left) A pre-classic double vase in the shape of a coati. (Below) A classic three-legged dish.

Pottery

Mayan pottery began with single-color objects. During the classic period, multicolored objects were made and painted. These were followed by vessels covered with scenes from life as well as geometric designs. In addition to containers of various shapes and sizes, Mayan potters concentrated mainly on figurines, incense burners, and whistles.

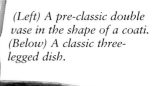

In this wall painting, Toltec warriors in canoes approach a Mayan coastal village.

Schools and learning

Among the class of scribes, young men were taught to understand and then write Mayan hieroglyphs (as shown above). This was very special knowledge, shared by few. Among ordinary families, girls were taught by their mothers how to cook, weave, and look after the household. Boys learned farming and hunting skills from their fathers. The children of potters and other craftworkers were also taught their parents' special skills.

Women

Mayan women and their older daughters cooked, looked after the young children, and collected firewood and water for the house. They also made the family's clothes, weaving cloth on looms (see below). This gave them a chance to meet other women, since they sometimes gathered in a village building that was set aside for weaving. Most women used sisal (made of fibers from the agave plant) and bark cloth, while richer families had cotton.

Earrings made of polished jadeite, from Copán.

(Below) A necklace from the late-classic period.

Trade

Mayan cities had a central market, where people of the region could come to exchange goods. The Maya of the highlands also traded with those in the lowlands, carrying goods on their backs or sometimes travelling along rivers in dugout canoes. The Mayan lands contained many natural resources that were of interest to other people, such as those who lived in the Mexican highlands. These included salt, honey, cacao, animal skins, bird feathers, and obsidian.

A group of merchants with their guardian god, Ek Chuah ("Black Scorpion"). He was also the patron of cacao, one of the merchants' most important products.

Clothing and jewelry

Since it was usually warm in their homelands, the Maya had simple, comfortable clothes. Men wore a loincloth—a strip of material wound around the waist and between the legs. Women wore long, loose, short-sleeved dresses. If the weather turned cold, both men and women put on a cloak. The Maya wore leather sandals on their feet (below), with different designs for special occasions. Early jewelry was made of shells and jaguar teeth; later it was fashioned from precious stones and metals.

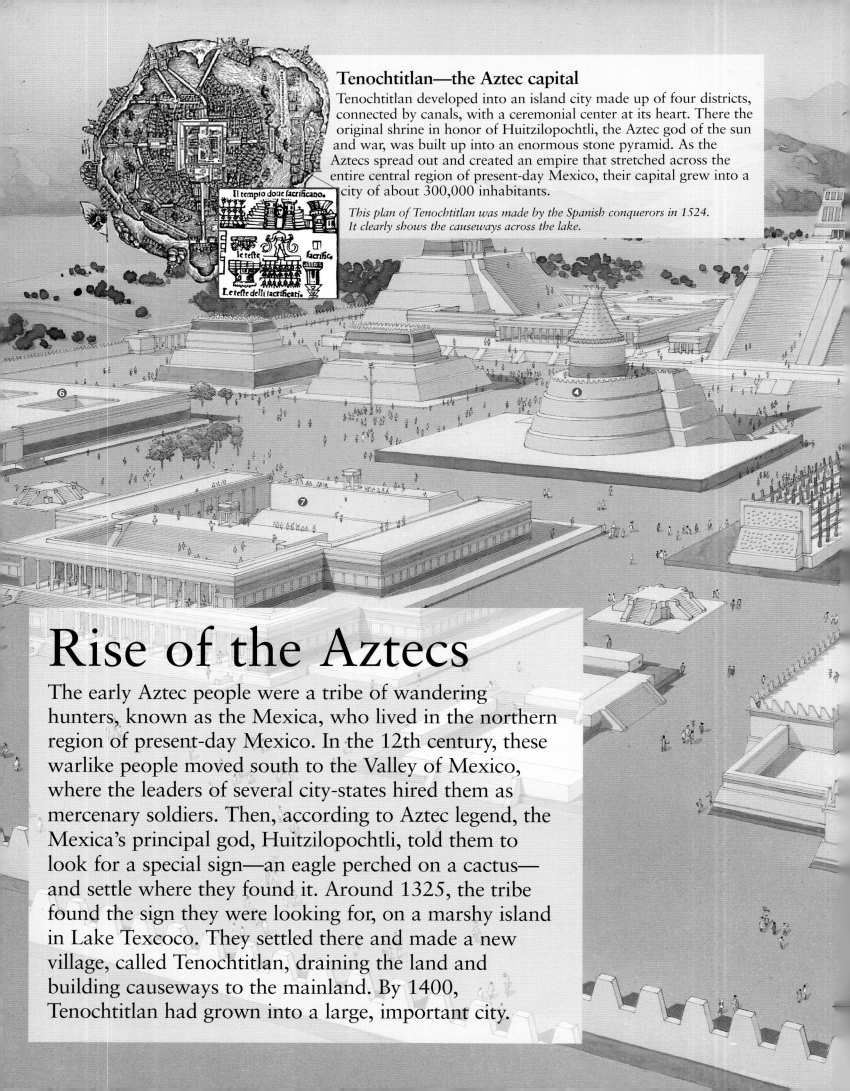

Tenochtitlan—the Aztec capital

Tenochtitlan developed into an island city made up of four districts, connected by canals, with a ceremonial center at its heart. There the original shrine in honor of Huitzilopochtli, the Aztec god of the sun and war, was built up into an enormous stone pyramid. As the Aztecs spread out and created an empire that stretched across the entire central region of present-day Mexico, their capital grew into a city of about 300,000 inhabitants.

This plan of Tenochtitlan was made by the Spanish conquerors in 1524. It clearly shows the causeways across the lake.

Rise of the Aztecs

The early Aztec people were a tribe of wandering hunters, known as the Mexica, who lived in the northern region of present-day Mexico. In the 12th century, these warlike people moved south to the Valley of Mexico, where the leaders of several city-states hired them as mercenary soldiers. Then, according to Aztec legend, the Mexica's principal god, Huitzilopochtli, told them to look for a special sign—an eagle perched on a cactus— and settle where they found it. Around 1325, the tribe found the sign they were looking for, on a marshy island in Lake Texcoco. They settled there and made a new village, called Tenochtitlan, draining the land and building causeways to the mainland. By 1400, Tenochtitlan had grown into a large, important city.

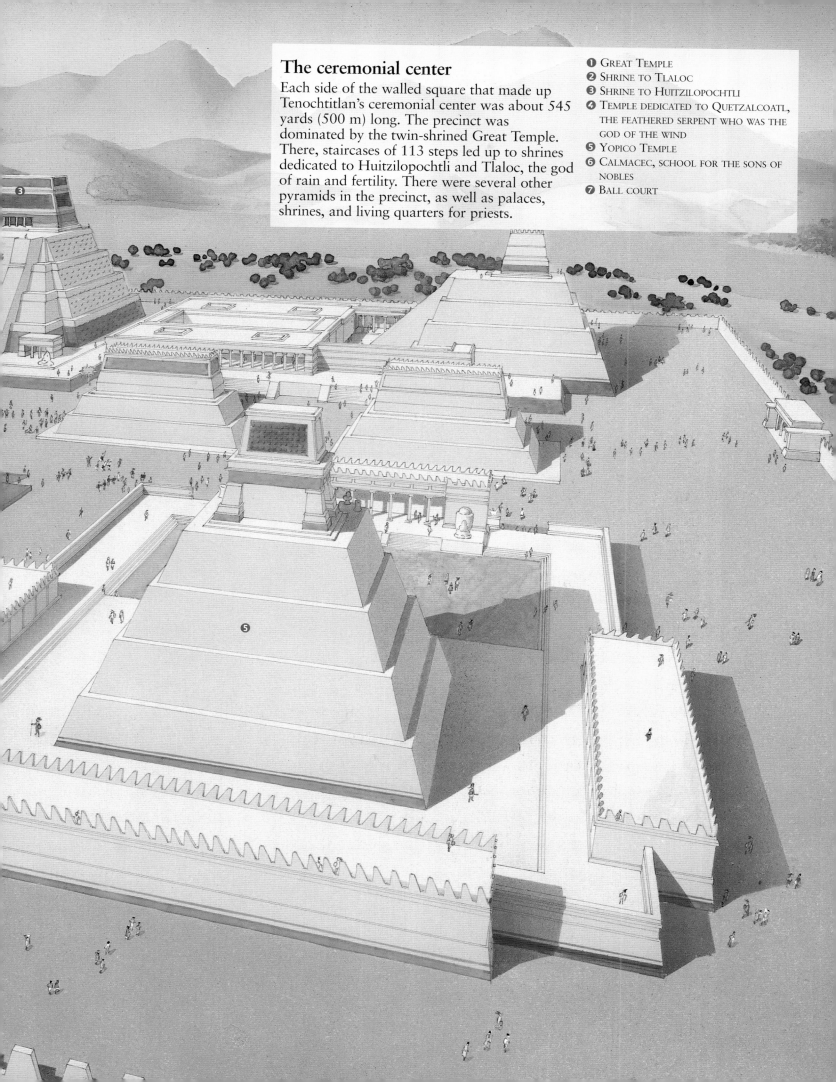

The ceremonial center

Each side of the walled square that made up Tenochtitlan's ceremonial center was about 545 yards (500 m) long. The precinct was dominated by the twin-shrined Great Temple. There, staircases of 113 steps led up to shrines dedicated to Huitzilopochtli and Tlaloc, the god of rain and fertility. There were several other pyramids in the precinct, as well as palaces, shrines, and living quarters for priests.

❶ GREAT TEMPLE
❷ SHRINE TO TLALOC
❸ SHRINE TO HUITZILOPOCHTLI
❹ TEMPLE DEDICATED TO QUETZALCOATL, THE FEATHERED SERPENT WHO WAS THE GOD OF THE WIND
❺ YOPICO TEMPLE
❻ CALMACEC, SCHOOL FOR THE SONS OF NOBLES
❼ BALL COURT

Aztec Villages

Aztec villages grew up near the fields farmed by the men. Many were small settlements, housing no more than 50 families. The villagers' houses were simple, made of branches or reeds plastered with clay or of sun-dried mud bricks. Many families lived all together in one room, sitting and sleeping on woven reed mats on the hard, earth floor. As people became wealthier, they added separate rooms for washing and sleeping. Women spent all their time at home in the village, preparing food, spinning and weaving, and looking after the young children. The craftsmen of the village generally worked outdoors, though they probably built workshops in larger towns and cities.

Handicrafts

The Aztecs wove reed baskets that were used to carry and store grain and other produce. Skilled potters coiled strips of clay into vases and jars for storage. Although they did not use a potter's wheel or high-firing techniques, Aztec potters made striking ceramics for everyday use and ceremonies. Clothing was woven in the villages. Each Aztec region had its own distinctive designs and patterns.

Aztec Religion

The Aztecs believed that the world in which they lived was the fifth "sun," or era. The previous four eras, before humans were born, had been destroyed by wild animals, storms, fires, and floods. The Aztecs also believed that their own, fifth, era would eventually be destroyed by earthquakes. The Aztec world was controlled by many gods and goddesses, who needed human blood to remain strong and keep everything in order. It was for this reason that human sacrifice played an important part in all major religious ceremonies. Ceremonies were carried out by priests, who must have looked fearsome with their long, matted hair, but who held positions of great importance in Aztec society.

This mask of Tezcatlipoca was made by laying turquoise, obsidian, and gold pyrites over a human skull.

The priesthood

Priests not only controlled Aztec cults and rites, but they also governed schools and the artistic life of the empire. Most came from the class of nobles. The two head priests, who were next in rank to the Aztec ruler, were responsible for the cult of Huitzilopochtli and Tlaloc, whose shrines were on top of the Great Temple in Tenochtitlan. Some of the lower-rank priests were also warriors, and they carried idols of gods into battle. Women priests were responsible for the earth-mother cults and maize goddesses.

A priest probably wore this mosaic double-headed snake, which acted as a symbol of the sky.

Tlazolteotl, one of the earth goddesses, is shown giving birth.

The Aztec calendar

Like the Maya, the Aztecs had two calendars. The ritual calendar, or "counting of the days," had a 260-day cycle. This was used by priests to forecast future events and had great religious significance. The solar calendar, or "counting of the years," had 365 days and was used to determine regular seasonal festivals. The two calendars came together once every 52 years, when there were special ceremonies.

The Aztec Sun Stone (above), found beneath Mexico City in 1790, shows the face of the Sun God at its center. It is surrounded by symbols of the four earlier "suns" and the 20 named days of the ritual calendar.

This illustration shows the creator god and goddess, Ometecuhtli and Omecihuatl. They are sitting in a sacred enclosure, from which life-giving water is flowing.

Mythology

The Aztecs saw the earth as a circle, with the surrounding sea meeting the upturned bowl of the sky. They believed that human beings had been created at the beginning of their own, fifth world. There were many myths about creator gods. According to one, Quetzalcoatl (the feathered serpent) went down to the underworld and gathered a heap of bones. He sprinkled these with his own blood to create humans.

A sacrificial stone knife with a mosaic handle.

Human sacrifice

Sacrificial victims had to climb to the top of a temple pyramid. Priests then stretched each victim across a sacrificial stone. Another priest slashed open the victim's chest with a knife and tore out his heart, which was the most precious thing that could be offered to the gods. The heart was placed in a bowl, and the dead victim's body was thrown down the temple steps. Sometimes parts of the body were given as a reward to the victim's captor.

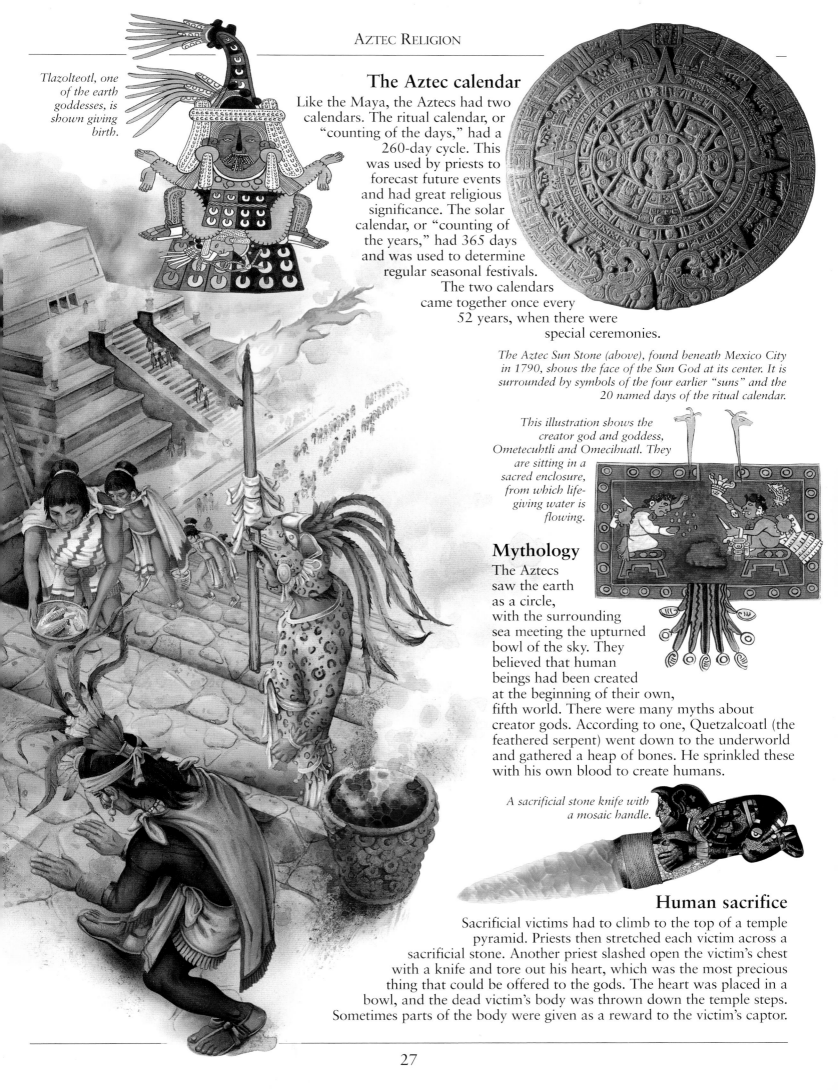

Aztec Life and Rituals

Aztec society was made up of four classes: nobles, commoners, serfs, and slaves. Among the nobles and commoners, individual families belonged to larger clans. Each clan had its own area of land, divided up among the families according to their needs. Commoners farmed their own land, while nobles had their work done by serfs. Most slaves were people who had fallen on hard times, and people could be sold into slavery if they had debts or were caught stealing. Most Aztec boys were trained at school to use weapons, and at the age of 15, they often went to war. They knew that successful warriors were always well rewarded, with gifts of land or slaves.

When a young couple wanted to marry, the bride was carried to the groom's house. The couple then sat together on a mat in front of the hearth, and the young man's cloak was tied to the bride's dress. The tying of the knot showed that they were married.

This toy (right) shows that the Aztecs understood the use of the wheel, though they did not use wheels for transport.

The Aztecs kept small dogs, which they fattened up to eat at special feasts.

Daily life

The Aztecs reclaimed land from swamps and lakes to make plots called chinampas, or "floating gardens." They kept piling up layers of mud in each plot until the level was above the surface of the water. They put human dung on their plots to fertilize the soil, which they tilled with long, pointed digging sticks. The Aztecs grew large crops of maize and vegetables, and the men and older boys worked very hard tending their plots.

Craftspeople

The Aztecs carved in stone, made baskets and pottery, and used feathers in brilliant ways. They hunted and raised birds in captivity for their feathers, and the beautiful green feathers of the quetzal bird were specially prized. Trained feather-workers glued and wove feathers together (right), often applying them to backing sheets of cotton. The results were spectacular fans, headdresses, and ornaments.

This beautiful feather fan has a bamboo handle.

Children

Aztec children had to help their parents with household chores. Small children gathered firewood and fetched water. Older children carried heavier loads to and from market. Boys helped their fathers with farming, and girls helped their mothers with cooking and weaving. Parents could be strict: a disobedient child might be scratched with thorns or even held over burning peppers to make his or her eyes sting.

The ball game

Like the Maya, the Aztecs played a special game on a ball court surrounded by high, sloping walls (below). Two teams of players tried to hit a solid rubber ball through a stone ring set high in the wall, and points may have been scored in other ways. The players hit the ball with their forearms, shoulders, elbows, or hips, and injuries were frequent. Though we call this a "game," historians believe that it often formed part of a religious event or sacred ritual.

Warriors and war

Boys were trained at school to use weapons, but there was no standing army. Warriors were called up for specific campaigns. Most of their weapons were made of wood, and they used obsidian to make spikes and blades. Warriors had slings, spears, and bows and arrows, and at close quarters they wielded wooden, clublike swords with obsidian blades. Some warriors wore quilted cotton suits, which were soaked in salt water to make them stiff and armor- like.

Terracotta figure of an eagle warrior. Eagle and jaguar warriors made up two special military orders. This warrior's helmet is shaped like an eagle's beak, and he wears wings on his arms.

Chavín culture

The Chavín culture, which was at its height from about 900 to 200 B.C., was the most widespread early culture in the Andean region. It is named after the highland ceremonial center of Chavín de Huántar, in present-day Peru, where there was a large temple complex. The Chavín people worshipped jaguars, eagles, and snakes as gods, and their art featured stylized animals. They were also expert metalworkers.

Paracas and Nazca

An ancient cemetery has been discovered at Paracas, suggesting that there was a culture there around the end of the Chavín period. Those people may well have been the ancestors of the Nazca, who lived in a desert region near the coast. The Nazca, who flourished from about 200 B.C. to A.D. 700, built underground aqueducts to bring water to the desert and turn it into farmland. They also drew lines in the desert in amazing shapes, which have remained a mystery to this day. Some historians believe there was a link between the Nazca Lines and water supplies.

The Chavín carved figures on the stone walls of their temples. This carving shows a warrior with an ax.

Below: This ceramic bowl shows Moche metalworkers blowing into a brazier to raise the temperature of the charcoal fire.

Moche civilization

From about A.D. 100 to 800, the Moche people built kingdoms along the northern coast. They were expert potters and metalworkers, irrigating dry valleys and fishing in the ocean from reed boats. Their rulers collected taxes in the form of labor, which helped build roads that lasted until Incan times. The Moche also built mud-brick pyramids and platforms, which served as religious and administrative centers.

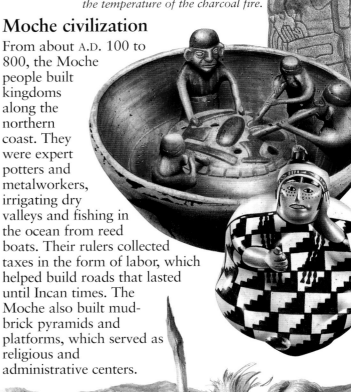

Before the Incas

In the northern Andes

At the northern end of the Andes mountains, in modern Colombia, many groups were organized into small chiefdoms. The San Agustín culture, which began around 500 B.C., left giant figures carved of stone. Peoples such as the Calima, Chibcha, and Sinú were all good potters, sculptors, and metalworkers. The Tairona built hundreds of terraced villages in the forested foothills. The Quimbaya, who lived around the headwaters of the river Cauca, became expert goldsmiths.

Opposite: Ceramic pot in the shape of a Nazca woman chewing coca leaves. Andean people did this to help overcome tiredness and hunger.

Above: This gold pendant from the Quimbaya region of Colombia may have been worn by a shaman.

Tribes of hunter-gatherers were roaming the mountains, rainforests, and deserts of South America by 11,000 B.C., or even earlier. This was a time of climate change, and as ice melted and the weather got warmer, some groups settled in the Andes and along the Pacific coast. They farmed the land and built villages. And from about 1000 B.C., several different cultures developed. Small civilizations rose and fell over the next 2,000 years, including those of the Chavín, Nazca, and Moche peoples. They each developed methods of farming and running their societies that were to influence the Incas. The last of the pre-Inca cultures, the Chimu, treated their rulers as god-kings and worshipped them even after their death. The Incas conquered the Chimu and adopted many of their ways.

This map of western South America shows where the pre-Inca peoples lived.

- Chavín de Huántar
- Chan Chan
- Cuzco
- *LAKE TITICACA*
- Tiwanaku

Huari and Tiwanaku

The city of Tiwanaku, just south of Lake Titicaca, was founded around A.D. 500 and was at its height 300 years later. This great ceremonial center had pyramids, palaces, and temples, and may have had a population of up to 60,000. Tiwanaku culture spread south into present-day Bolivia and Chile. The nearby Wari people, on the other hand, moved north. They were great road-builders and kept records with knotted strings, just as the Inca would later.

This gold and turquoise figure was made in the Sicán region and taken by the Chimu.

The Chimu

Beginning around A.D. 800, the Chimu built an empire that was the largest in the region before the Incas. Their capital of Chan Chan, on the Pacific coast, was an enormous city made of adobe. It was full of craftworkers and traders. The Chimu expanded their empire through warfare, becoming rivals to the nearby Incas. Around 1470, the Incas finally conquered the Chimu. They plundered Chan Chan and carried off skilled Chimu workers.

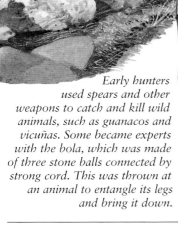

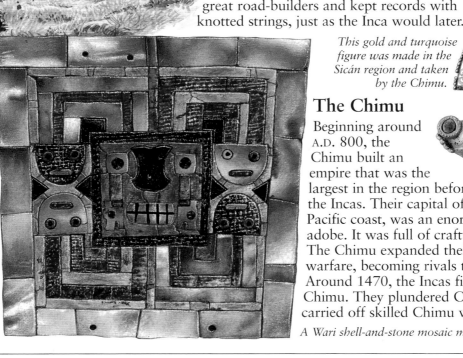

Early hunters used spears and other weapons to catch and kill wild animals, such as guanacos and vicuñas. Some became experts with the bola, which was made of three stone balls connected by strong cord. This was thrown at an animal to entangle its legs and bring it down.

A Wari shell-and-stone mosaic mirror.

Grave goods

It was the Incan custom to place various items in graves. These would be useful to the dead person in the afterlife. The quality and amount of goods varied with the social status of the individual. Some men were given weapons and hunting tools, while women often had their work-baskets buried with them. Food and drink were also offered, along with pottery vessels. Gold and silver objects were placed in the tombs of high-ranking people.

This gold figurine was found in a grave. Human and animal figurines were often buried as religious offerings.

Clothing formed an important part of many burials. This beautiful Incan tunic is made of alpaca wool delicately covered with tiny sheets of gold.

Incan Burial

Since respect for ancestors and the dead was important to the Incas, they took great trouble with their burial methods. These varied according to the wealth and importance of the deceased person, as well as location. The Incas knew that dead bodies would be well preserved in very dry or cold conditions. In the mountains, bodies were placed in caves or rocky niches. Some were even placed high above the snow line, at the very top of a mountain. In the lowlands, ordinary people were placed in holes in the sandy ground. Some were put in stone vaults covered with sticks and leaves. Wealthier people were given tombs. Most burials were accompanied by offerings to the gods.

This tapestry shows the flying figure of a shaman, who was thought to be in contact with the spirit world of the dead.

Funerals

The Incas held funerals, but not much is known about their funeral rituals, as much evidence was destroyed by the Spanish invaders. Certainly rulers and other important individuals were buried with great ceremony, and some of their wives and servants were killed so that they could accompany them into the afterlife. Funerals were sad occasions, and some women mourners cut off their long hair to show their grief. There was slow music accompanied by a funeral dance.

Tombs

Important Incas were buried in stone chambers, or tombs. A ruler was often laid in a special room inside his palace.

The handle of this ceramic vessel is decorated with a human figure. The pot served as an offering at an Incan burial and was found in a large cemetery near Lima, Peru.

CAPITVLO PRIMERO ENTIERO

INCAILLAPA AIA DEF

pvcv llo

yllapa oquinto

This illustration shows water being poured as part of a funeral rite for an important person, possibly a ruler. It was drawn by the 17th-century Andean writer Guamán Poma de Ayala.

Incan Religion

Religion played an important part in the everyday lives of the Incas. They believed that their world had been made by a god called Viracocha, the "old man of the sky." He had created people out of stone. Viracocha had also made all the other gods, including the most important— Inti, the sun god. The Incas believed that Inti, the divine ancestor of their ruler, sank into the western ocean each evening, swam all the way beneath the earth, and then reappeared in the eastern sky the next morning. There was a great temple dedicated to the sun in Cuzco, where thousands of priests, priestesses, and attendants helped worship their greatest deity. Priests were also important in daily life, for they used their special knowledge to foretell events, predicting the outcome of battles and diagnosing illnesses.

Inti was often represented as a golden face surrounded by a sunburst. This image was used for face masks worn at special festivals.

Ceramic figurine of a priest pouring water as part of a religious ritual.

This ceramic vase shows a row of women in shawls and long dresses. They may have been priestesses, who served as ceremonial brides of the gods.

This silver figurine was found near the body of a boy who may have been sacrificed to the sun god. The magnificent feather headdress, woolen cloak, and silver pin suggest that the figure may represent a god.

Gods and goddesses

There were many important gods and goddesses in addition to the creator god Viracocha and the sun god Inti. Farmers addressed many of their prayers to Apu Illapu, the god of thunder and giver of rain. In times of drought, they made pilgrimages to temples dedicated to him. Inti's sister and wife, Mamakilya, was the goddess of the moon. She was associated with silver, which was thought to be made of the tears of the moon. The deities of the earth and sea were also female.

Priests

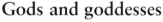

Priests played a vital role in Incan society, especially since important decisions were based on what they foretold. The chief priest in Cuzco, who was always a nobleman related to the ruler (often his brother or uncle), held the highest position. He appointed other high priests, who were trained in religious ritual and looked after temples in the 10 religious districts of the empire. They were helped by chosen women, who prepared food for religious ceremonies and made fine clothes for the royal family and high priests.

Sacred places

Many different places were sacred to the Incas. These sacred sites (or huacas) included temples and other holy places, as well as natural features such as mountain peaks and rocks. The city of Machu Picchu (right) was surrounded by sacred places: mountain peaks to the north and south, and the Urubamba River, with its life-giving water, in the valley below.

The ruins of Machu Picchu were rediscovered in 1911. The city contained a small sacred plaza, as well as a circular Temple of the Sun.

Mummies

Preserved bodies, made up as mummy bundles, were treated with great respect. The mummy of a ruler, dressed in magnificent clothes, was kept in the royal palace and looked after by his descendants. On special festival days, a royal mummy would often be taken out of the palace and carried through the streets (below). In this way, the former ruler could continue to enjoy festivals, and citizens had the opportunity to worship him.

Rituals

The Incas marked the changing seasons and important state occasions with religious rituals and festivals. In important centers, such as Cuzco, priests started the day with prayers and offerings to the gods. There may have been as many as 150 festivals each year. One of the most important was a midwinter festival called the Feast of the Sun, which was held to celebrate life-giving light and warmth.

This silver statuette of a llama was found near a Sun Temple on an island in Lake Titicaca. Llamas, especially pure white ones, were regularly used for sacrifice.

ROADS

Incan Roads and Trade

The territory of the Inca empire, known as Tahuantinsuyu ("Land of the Four Quarters"), was crisscrossed with thousands of miles of roads. These formed a well-maintained network for the use of all those on official business. The roads were used to transport goods, move conquered subjects closer to the capital (where they could be more closely watched), send troops quickly to the ends of the empire, and link Cuzco and the Inca ruler with both the highlands and the coast. They also formed an excellent communications network. Royal messengers ran along the roads between special stone shelters, where they passed their message on to the next relay runner. In this way, messages could travel up to 155 miles (250 km) a day. On the main roads, there were rest-houses for travellers at regular intervals.

The map shows the two main roads that ran north-south. One ran along the spine of the Andes mountains, the other along the coast. There were many smaller, connecting roads.

The roads system

The main routes spread out from Cuzco. These were wide, paved roads up to 50 feet (15 m) across. Other, smaller routes were made up of simple paths just over six feet (2 m) wide. Many of these had been taken over from earlier, pre-Inca peoples. The roads, bridges, and tunnels were built by ordinary Inca subjects as part of the labor tax that they had to pay to the state.

Where possible, the roads were flat, but mountain roads were stepped. Ravines, some more than 130 feet (40 m) across, were crossed by rope bridges.

Transporting goods

Since the Incas had no wheeled vehicles, travellers walked. They led caravans of llamas to carry their goods, which they loaded into state storehouses along the way. Other items of baggage were carried by human porters. Nobles did not have to go on foot: they rode in litters, which were carried on men's shoulders.

Statuette of a man carrying a large jar on his back. The long, narrow neck helped prevent spills of the liquid inside, which may have been chicha (maize beer).

Woven bags such as this were used to carry coca leaves.

Administering the state

The Inca state was highly centralized, with a strict hierarchy. Immediately beneath the ruler were the prefects of the Four Quarters. Then came provincial governors, district officers, and local chiefs. At the bottom of the administrative pyramid, foremen supervised groups of 10 families, who had to contribute some of their labor as a tax to the state. Since there was no system of writing, government officials kept records with the help of a complex calculator called a quipu.

The quipu was a series of strings tied to a cord. Knots were used to represent numbers within a decimal system. Different positions and clusters of knots meant different numbers. Experts also used the quipu to help them remember lists and other facts.

Trade

The Inca state controlled most trade, especially the trading of precious metals such as gold and silver. Ordinary people could exchange foodstuffs and textiles at local fairs. There was no system of money, so goods were exchanged. People from the mountains were able to exchange freeze-dried potatoes and meat for lowland produce such as maize, cotton, beans, and salt. Pottery goods and animals, such as guinea pigs, were also traded.

Water transport

The Incas used reed boats to travel on lakes and rivers. The reeds, gathered from the shores of lakes, were bound in tight bundles and then bent into curved shapes. For sailing along the coast, the Incas built balsa-wood rafts. These could be used to transport heavy cargo and army supplies.

This balsa-wood raft has a single canvas sail and a wooden steering oar. The cabin was made of bamboo, roofed with banana leaves.

Terraced fields

In the mountains, the Incas created flat farming land by turning the slopes into terraces (left). They built retaining walls at the top of each terrace so that the earth would not be washed away during rainstorms. They put down stones to help drainage and then placed soil on top. Some of the soil had to be brought up from fertile valleys below. Irrigation channels were dug, connecting the fields to rivers and streams so that they could be watered in the dry season. The Incas even bored through rock to make channels from springs.

Farming methods

Springtime meant lots of hard work for the whole farming family. Before sowing seeds, men dug and turned the earth with a tool called a taclla, or foot plow. This was a long pole with a foot-rest above a point of fire-hardened wood or bronze. Women then broke up the soil with hoes. Farmers also fertilized their fields, using llama dung in the mountains and seabird droppings near the coast.

(Above) A wooden hoe. (Right) A pitchfork. (Far right) A ceremonial taclla, or foot plow, decorated with a corn cob and a jug for maize beer.

Incan Farmers

The Incas were accomplished farmers. They used irrigation to turn dry and mountainous terrain into flat, fertile fields. Every married man was given an allotment of land that was just big enough to support his immediate family. Extended families were grouped together in small communities, and they had to work land that was set aside for the emperor and priests, as well as their own. But most families had enough food. They ate two meals a day, one early in the morning and the second just before sunset. Most meals consisted of stews made with maize, potatoes, beans, squash, and hot chilies. Some meat was eaten, and fish was popular, especially near the coast and lakes. There were lots of tropical fruits, including pineapples, guavas, and papayas. After a meal, the Incas liked to drink maize beer.

This dish was probably used for offerings in harvest rituals. It was found with the remains of corn cobs from Incan times. Potatoes are the tubers of a root crop. More than 200 varieties were grown in the Andes.

Food

Potatoes and maize were the Incas' most important crops. Potatoes, which were first grown around the region of Lake Titicaca, were also freeze-dried to make food called chuño. This was done by leaving the tubers out in the nighttime frost and then letting them dry out in the hot sun. The pressed chuño could be kept and then soaked in water before cooking. Another important food was a porridge made from the boiled seeds of quinoa, a tough plant which grows well in the highlands and is sometimes called "mountain rice."

Fishing on Lake Titicaca, which lies high in the Andes. The Incas ate many different kinds of fresh fish caught in lakes, rivers, and the sea. They also preserved fish by salting and drying it.

Ceremonial vessel in the shape of a fish, dating from around 1500.

Animals

The Incas kept guinea pigs for their meat, which they roasted. Herds of llamas were also kept, and their meat was sometimes eaten. It was cut into thin strips, dried, and then pounded between stones to make a preserved meat known as charqui. But llamas were too valuable as beasts of burden and sources of wool to be used as everyday food.

These three animals all belong to the camel family. The llama (left) is the largest and was domesticated along with the alpaca (above), represented here by a silver statuette. The wild vicuña (top) is the smallest and has the shortest hair.

Taxes

Ordinary men and women paid taxes to the state by working in the fields that produced food for priests and the emperor. Up to two-thirds of a farmer's time might be spent in this way, and the religious and imperial lands were always dug, planted, and harvested first. After the harvest, the state produce was hauled off to special storehouses. This meant that there was always plenty of food for the many Incan festivals or in times of drought.

On an inspection of storehouses, the emperor (right) is given information by an official with a quipu calculator.

DEPOCITODELINGA COLL CA

Life in the Mountains

One of the most astonishing things about the ancient Incas is that so many of them lived at very high altitudes. Yet they still managed to farm, trade, travel, develop advanced irrigation and engineering projects, and maintain a rich social and religious life. This illustration shows how the Incas made use of every square inch of mountaintop and how they terraced the steep slopes.

The Inca Empire

Around 1100, the Incas were simply one of many small tribes in the Andes. According to legend, their first emperor was called Manko Qapaq, and his successor took the title Sapa Inca, or "Only Leader." Six more emperors ruled before Pachacuti came to power in 1438. By then, rivalries had sprung up within the royal family, but Pachacuti was able to reunite the empire. Throughout this period, the empire grew quickly, and at its height there were about 12 million Inca subjects. Of these, fewer than 40,000 were of Incan blood, yet this amazing group of people was able to build the greatest Andean empire.

This plan of Cuzco shows the general layout. Four main roads led out of the city, heading for the "four quarters" of the empire. At the top, a fortress overlooks the city.

This jar has an Incan shape that was standard throughout the empire. Differences in design showed which province an item came from. This jar is painted in the Chimu style.

This golden royal raft comes from the northern Andes. Pieces such as this from around the Inca Empire helped create mythical tales of El Dorado (see page 45).

Cuzco—the capital

In the Quechua language of the Incas, "Cuzco" means "navel." Their capital city was so named because the Incas saw it as the navel, or center, of the world. Cuzco lies in the Peruvian Andes, at a height of 11,500 feet (3,500 m). It was founded around 1100 by Manko Qapaq, and later rebuilt as the imperial capital by Pachacuti. It was a magnificent city, with many fountains and underground drains. The Temple of the Sun stood beside the city's central plaza, near the emperor's palace.

This unfortunate individual, probably a thief, had the skin flayed from his face before he was tied to a tree.

Organization of the state

Tahuantinsuyu (the "Land of the Four Quarters") was organized into 80 provinces. This vast territory included many different peoples and languages, so the Incas made their own—Quechua—the official spoken language of the empire. There was, of course, no written language. In the outlying provinces, conquered chiefs became important imperial subjects. They were educated in Incan ways and then allowed to keep their local powers.

The emperor is surrounded by his courtiers in the center of Cuzco, which was itself the center of the Inca Empire.

End of the empire

When Emperor Huayna Qapaq died without a chosen successor in about 1527, two of his sons fought for the position. Huascar took the title in Cuzco, but his brother Atahualpa controlled a large army to the north. Eventually, Atahualpa defeated his brother and became emperor in 1532. The civil war severely weakened the empire, allowing Spanish invaders to conquer it easily (see pages 44–45).

Wooden ax and club with stone heads; the star was attached to a strap and whirled around to knock out the enemy.

The military power

The Incas used great military force to build and then hold together their empire. They had a standing army of around 10,000 troops, but at any one time it was much larger than this. Ordinary farmers had to join the army for a time. This counted as part of their tax payment to the state, along with road-building and farmwork. Soldiers were armed with clubs, battleaxes, spears, and slings. They wore quilted cotton armor and carried wooden shields.

Rules and regulations

State officials throughout the provinces made sure that all subjects obeyed Incan laws. Everyone had to pay their taxes (mostly in the form of labor), and officials checked the size of family farming plots and their yield. Conquered chiefs often acted as judges in the provinces. Stealing from official storehouses was a serious crime, and anyone found guilty faced the death penalty. Less serious crimes were punished by various forms of torture or exile from the empire.

THE AZTECS, INCAS, & MAYA

Index